BLACK
ACHIEVEMENTS
IN ENTERTAINMENT

**CELEBRATING HATTIE MCDANIEL,
CHADWICK BOSEMAN, AND MORE**

**ELLIOTT SMITH
CICELY LEWIS, EXECUTIVE EDITOR**

Lerner Publications ◆ Minneapolis

LETTER FROM CICELY LEWIS

Dear Reader,

As a girl, I wanted to be like Oprah Winfrey. She is a Black woman from Mississippi like me who became an award-winning actor, author, and businessperson. Oftentimes, history books leave out the accomplishments and contributions of people of color. When you

CICELY LEWIS

see someone who looks like you and has a similar background excelling at something, it helps you to see yourself be great.

I created Read Woke to amplify the voices of people who are often underrepresented. These books bring to light the beauty, talent, and integrity of Black people in music, activism, sports, the arts, and other areas. As you read, think about why it's important to celebrate Black excellence and the achievements of all people regardless of race, gender, or status. How did the people mentioned succeed despite barriers placed on them? How can we use these stories to inspire others?

Black excellence is everywhere in your daily life. I hope these people inspire you to never give up and continue to let your light shine.

With gratitude,

Cicely Lewis

TABLE OF CONTENTS

GONE TOO SOON

From Jackie Robinson to Thurgood Marshall, actor Chadwick Boseman stepped into the shoes of many Black heroes on film. Many believe he became a hero himself after portraying Black Panther in the groundbreaking movie of the same name. His powerful performance moved and inspired millions of people. His future as a performer seemed bright.

Sadly, Boseman died of cancer in 2020. But his legacy will not be forgotten. He had many iconic performances, none bigger than T'Challa in *Black Panther*. Howard University, the college he went to, recognized his talent by renaming its College of Fine Arts after him.

Entertainers do much more than make us laugh or cry. They inspire audiences young and old. This book will explore Black excellence throughout entertainment. While not every important entertainer is in this book, the ones highlighted have helped shape or change entertainment.

Boseman smiles while attending the US *Black Panther* premiere.

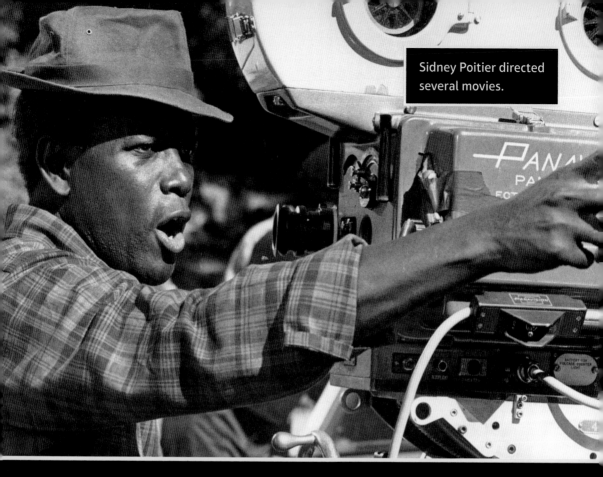

Sidney Poitier directed several movies.

CHAPTER 1
PIONEERS

For early entertainers, finding success in show business was hard. Many Black performers faced racism. They worked hard to build solid careers. And they led the way for other entertainers to follow.

OSCAR OUTCAST

Hattie McDaniel was one of the few Black women to make gains in early Hollywood. She took roles she didn't agree with but always said she'd rather play a maid than be one. Her most successful part came in the 1939 movie *Gone with the Wind*. The next year, McDaniel won the Oscar for Best Supporting Actress, making her the first Black actor to win an Oscar.

McDaniel accepted her award from a segregated table at the ceremony. The seating showed the hardships such as racism that she faced. But McDaniel continued to act until her death in 1952.

Hattie McDaniel showing off her award for *Gone with the Wind*

REFLECT

ACTING LEGEND

Sidney Poitier was electric on-screen. Black actors were often forced to play supporting characters, but Poitier remained powerful. By the late 1950s, Poitier emerged as the first Black actor to earn starring roles in the US. He helped end many on-screen taboos for Black actors, such as romantic relationships between a Black character and a white character. Poitier became the first Black man to win a Best Actor Oscar with his role in the 1963 movie *Lilies of the Field*.

Poitier later became a successful director. He was also a civil rights activist. President Barack Obama awarded him the Presidential Medal of Freedom in 2009. Poitier's poise and strength motivated generations of Black entertainers.

> "In order for others to come behind me, there were certain things I had to do."
>
> —SIDNEY POITIER, IN A 2000 INTERVIEW WITH OPRAH WINFREY FOR *O, THE OPRAH MAGAZINE*

Sidney Poitier received his first Oscar in 1964.

MUST-SEE TV

Ethel Waters became one of the first Black performers to find Broadway success. In 1939 she broke another barrier, this time in television. TV was new. NBC was trying to figure out how it would work. Executives asked Waters to perform content from her play on a TV program. *The Ethel Waters Show* was a one-time, one-hour variety show. Waters was likely the first Black person to ever appear on TV.

Waters made more TV history in the 1950s. She was the first Black woman to star in a TV series, *Beulah*. And in 1962, she became the first Black woman nominated for an Emmy.

Ethel Waters around 1944

REFLECT

What would you do if you were offered a part in a movie or show that didn't represent your race or culture positively?

DID YOU KNOW?

Pearl Bailey was another of the first Black stars on Broadway. She found success after Waters, first appearing on Broadway in 1946. She later became a Goodwill Ambassador to the United Nations. President Richard Nixon called her America's Ambassador of Love.

Pearl Bailey was an actor and singer.

Queen Latifah
performing in 1993

CHAPTER 2

TOTAL TALENTS

S ome entertainers are so talented that they succeed no matter the format. Whether acting, writing, or directing, these multitalented performers prove there's no one way to become a star.

ALL HAIL THE QUEEN

Queen Latifah started her entertainment journey as a rapper. She won a Grammy for her hit song "U.N.I.T.Y." in 1994. But music wasn't her only talent. She starred in the sitcom *Living Single* from 1993 to 1998. And she started a successful movie career, including roles in hits like the 2007 musical movie *Hairspray*.

Queen Latifah continues to move throughout the entertainment industry, starring in TV shows, recording music albums, and

producing movies. She became the first hip-hop artist to receive a star on the Hollywood Walk of Fame in 2006. In 2022 she was working in TV again.

Queen Latifah grins with her star on the Hollywood Walk of Fame.

DID YOU KNOW?

Marsai Martin is credited as the youngest executive producer in Hollywood history. The *Black-ish* actor came up with the idea for the film *Little* when she was ten. She was fourteen when the film was released.

QUADRUPLE THREAT

Harry Belafonte is an entertainment legend. He's reached amazing heights as a singer, songwriter, activist, and actor. His world-famous "Day-O (Banana Boat Song)" helped his album *Calypso* become the first record by a single artist to sell one million copies. He starred in several movies with friend Sidney Poitier. And he produced *Beat Street*, one of the first hip-hop movies.

Belafonte was a pioneer in the civil rights movement of the 1950s and 1960s. He often combined pop culture and politics in his work. He helped create the song "We Are the World" in 1985 to raise money for African famine relief. Belafonte joined the Rock and Roll Hall of Fame in 2022.

Harry Belafonte sings onstage in 1959. He sang many
types of music, including folk and blues.

VERY SECURE

Issa Rae first gained notice by writing and starring in a web show. A web show is made and posted online instead of airing on TV. The show went viral. Rae then wrote a best-selling memoir.

Rae moved from web shows to television. Her work captures the reality of young Black life. She writes, produces, and even directs. And Rae isn't done yet. Her production company, Hoorae, is developing multiple shows. She's even branching out into cartoons. Rae was picked to voice Spider-Woman in the 2023 *Spider-Man: Across the Spider-Verse.*

Issa Rae speaking at a 2016 event

REFLECT

What would your idea for a movie be? Who would star in it?

CHAPTER 3

POWERHOUSES

The greatest entertainers are easy to spot. They deliver performances or create works that win awards, make lasting memories for viewers, or break new ground. These entertainers aren't afraid to use their power to help other Black entertainers shine.

> "Acting is like music. . . . There's no rhyme or reason to it. . . . It's just a rhythm."
>
> —DENZEL WASHINGTON, IN A 2008 INTERVIEW

THE ACTOR'S ACTOR

Denzel Washington is one of the greatest actors ever. He's been nominated for ten Oscars and won two. Washington is one of just five male actors to be nominated for an Oscar in five different decades. He has played several memorable characters. And he's a well-respected director.

Washington supports the arts at all levels. For nearly thirty years, he has been the national spokesperson for the Boys & Girls Clubs of America. The organization provides after-school programs for children. His son John David Washington has followed in his footsteps by acting in films.

Denzel Washington (*left*) and his son John David Washington both act in movies.

LATE BLOOMER

For many years, actor Viola Davis played mostly supporting roles. But in the 2000s, Davis began earning bigger roles and awards that showed her skill. In 2017 Davis became the first Black woman to win an Oscar, Emmy, and Tony.

Davis is known as one of the best actors of the century. She does other work too. She founded JuVee Productions with her husband to create stronger roles and stories for Black actors and other actors of color. And she wrote a best-selling book that details her road to stardom.

Viola Davis with her husband, Julius Tennon, at the 2021 Academy Awards

Davis won her first Oscar in 2017.

THE VISIONARY

A great director like Spike Lee is fearless and bold. His ground-breaking work from behind the camera has transformed modern film. Lee's movies cover all aspects of Black experiences, from history to jazz to activism. Lee also directed several documentaries. And his Air Jordan TV commercials made basketball star Michael Jordan more famous.

Lee has showcased many talents during his long career, including acting, producing, and writing. He won his first Oscar for Best Adapted Screenplay in 2019. Lee helps teach the next wave of directors as a professor at New York University.

Spike Lee (*right*) directs Denzel Washington. Part of a director's job is telling actors what to do while filming.

REFLECT

How do directors shape a movie? Would you rather be an actor or a director?

CHAPTER 4

FRESH VOICES

There are always new people ready to share their talent with the world. These superstars are among the next wave of talented Black performers reshaping entertainment.

A TO Z

At just twenty-six, Zendaya was already one of the brightest stars in show business. She started her career as a teenager on Disney Channel shows such as *Shake It Up* and *K.C. Undercover*. From there, she turned to movies. She's costarred in several movies, including three *Spider-Man* films.

In 2020 she became the youngest woman to win an Emmy for Outstanding Lead Actress in a Drama Series. In 2022 she won another Emmy and became the youngest two-time acting winner. The fashion industry loves Zendaya too. She worked with designer Tommy Hilfiger on a 2019 clothing line. She models for several high fashion brands.

Zendaya won her second Emmy in 2022.

NOT SO CHILDISH

Comedy and music were both important to Donald Glover. He found a way to do both. Glover started with an internet sketch comedy group before costarring in the hit show *Community*. Glover started working on creating shows in addition to acting, and his TV fame grew. In 2018 he appeared in the sci-fi adventure film *Solo*.

Glover wanted his music to be separate from his acting. He used an online name generator to come up with the name Childish Gambino. He has released several popular albums and mixtapes. He won several Grammy Awards, including Record of the Year in 2019.

Childish Gambino has performed at several concerts and festivals.

REFLECT

Why do you think many actors are also successful musicians? Which do you think is harder, acting or singing?

Quinta Brunson attends the Streamy Awards in 2017. She left BuzzFeed the next year.

BUILDING A BUZZ

Quinta Brunson's success started small. She released funny shorts on Instagram. Then she got a job producing more comedy videos at the media company BuzzFeed. But Brunson had a specific project in mind. She left BuzzFeed in 2018 and began taking acting and writing jobs.

In 2021 she created *Abbott Elementary*, a comedy about teachers working in an inner-city school. Brunson stars in the show. It is based on her mother's teaching experiences. She even named the show after her own sixth-grade teacher! It became an immediate hit. Brunson is one of the hottest names in TV. Her story proves you can achieve your dreams no matter where you start.

Brunson (*right*) and her *Abbott Elementary* costar Sheryl Lee Ralph

DID YOU KNOW?

In 2003 Michael B. Jordan replaced Chadwick Boseman on the show *All My Children*. The actors later starred in *Black Panther* together.

FUTURE ENTERTAINMENT

Black entertainers continue to thrive. They break new ground in TV, in movies, and on Broadway. New writers and directors explore different Black experiences. These stories are creating an exciting time for entertainment. Check out some new actors and directors to discover what's next in entertainment and how the legacy of great Black performers continues.

GLOSSARY

ambassador: a person sent to represent their government in another country

famine: an extreme and long-term shortage of food

iconic: very famous or popular

memoir: a personal story based on the writer's own life

nominate: to choose as an option for an award or honor such as an Emmy or Oscar

producer: someone who helps create a movie or show by gathering money and talent

role: the part someone plays in a movie, TV show, or other kind of entertainment

segregated: when one group of people is separated from another based on their race

taboo: a social custom to avoid discussing or doing a certain activity

viral: quickly and widely spread or popularized

SOURCE NOTES

8   "Oprah Talks to Sydney Poitier," Oprah.com, accessed July 1, 2022, https://www.oprah.com/omagazine/oprah-interviews-sidney-poitier/3.

18 Terry Gross, "Denzel Washington: The *Fresh Air* Interview," NPR, July 8, 2022, https://www.npr.org/2022/07/08/1110475988/denzel-washington-the-fresh-air-interview.

READ WOKE READING LIST

Britannica Kids: Black Panther
https://kids.britannica.com/students/article/Black-Panther
/630865

Britannica Kids: Hattie McDaniel
https://kids.britannica.com/students/article/Hattie-McDaniel
/329561

Kiddle: Zendaya Facts for Kids
https://kids.kiddle.co/Zendaya

Norris, Hayley. *Donald Glover*. New York: Enslow, 2021.

Shea, Therese M. *Chadwick Boseman*. New York: PowerKids, 2022.

Smith, Elliott. *Black Achievements in Music: Celebrating Louis Armstrong, Beyoncé, and More*. Minneapolis: Lerner Publications, 2024.

Stark, Kristy. *Behind the Scenes with Marsai Martin*. Fremont, CA: Full Tilt, 2021.

INDEX

PHOTO ACKNOWLEDGMENTS

Images credits: Jeff Spicer/Getty Images, p. 4; Albert L. Ortega/Getty Images, p. 5; Silver Screen Collection/Getty Images, p. 6; Bettmann/Getty Images, p. 7; Archive Photos/Getty Images, p. 9; Michael Ochs Archives/Getty Images, p. 10; Afro American Newspapers/Gado/Getty Images, p. 11; Tim Mosenfelder/CORBIS/Getty Images, p. 12; Steve Granitz/Getty Images, p. 13; Hulton Archive/Getty Images, p. 15; Jerod Harris/WireImage/Getty Images, p. 16; M. Caulfield/WireImage/Getty Images, p. 17; Allen Berezovsky/Getty Images, p. 18; Matt Sayles/A.M.P.A.S./Getty Images, p. 19; Jeffrey Mayer/WireImage/Getty Images, p. 20; Mario Ruiz/Getty Images, p. 21; Mark Metcalfe/Getty Images, p. 22; David Livingston/Getty Images, p. 23; Jeff Kravitz/FilmMagic/Getty Images, p. 24; David Livingston/Getty Images, p. 25; JC Olivera/Getty Images, p. 26; Emma McIntyre/Getty Images, p. 27.

Cover: CBS Photo Archive/Getty Images; PA Images/Alamy Stock Photo.

Cecily Lewis portrait photos by Fernando Decillis.

Lerner Publications Company
An imprint of Lerner Publishing Group, Inc.
241 First Avenue North
Minneapolis, MN 55401 USA

For reading levels and more information, look up this title at www.lernerbooks.com.

Main body text set in Aptifer Sans LT Pro.
Typeface provided by Linotype AG.

Editor: Lauren Foley **Designer:** Kim Morales

Library of Congress Cataloging-in-Publication Data

Names: Smith, Elliott, 1976– author.
Title: Black achievements in entertainment : celebrating Hattie McDaniel, Chadwick Boseman, and more / Elliott Smith.
Description: Minneapolis : Lerner Publications, [2024] | Series: Black excellence project (read woke books) | Includes bibliographical references and index. | Audience: Ages 9–14 | Audience: Grades 4–6 | Summary: "Entertainers can make us laugh, cry, and everything in between. Explore how Black entertainers like Zendaya, Ethel Waters, and Donald Glover have influenced entertainment and inspired the next generation"—Provided by publisher.
Identifiers: LCCN 2022034604 (print) | LCCN 2022034605 (ebook) | ISBN 9781728486635 (library binding) | ISBN 9781728496221 (ebook)
Subjects: LCSH: African American entertainers—Juvenile literature. | African Americans in the performing arts—Juvenile literature.
Classification: LCC PN1590.B53 S65 2024 (print) | LCC PN1590.B53 (ebook) | DDC 791.089/96073—dc23/eng/20221209

LC record available at https://lccn.loc.gov/2022034604
LC ebook record available at https://lccn.loc.gov/2022034605

Manufactured in the United States of America
1-52593-50767-12/30/2022